IMAGES OF SCO

PORTOBELLO
AND DUDDINGSTON

To

Edna J. Jones

With best wishes from the authors
November 2005

Margaret Munro   Archie Foley

IMAGES OF SCOTLAND

PORTOBELLO
AND DUDDINGSTON

MARGARET MUNRO AND ARCHIE FOLEY

TEMPUS

Frontispiece: The coat of arms of Portobello Burgh Council featured sailing ships and cannons in its quarters in reference to Admiral Vernon's capture of Puerto Bella in Panama from the Spaniards in 1739. The crest denoted Portobello Tower, and a free rendering of the motto, *Ope et Consilio*, would be that success is achieved by hard work and taking sound advice. Grants of Arms are personal to the bearer so when the burgh council disappeared after Portobello amalgamated with Edinburgh in 1896, no other body could assume them. In 1996 Portobello Community Council successfully petitioned for new arms closely modelled on the old ones.

First published 2005

Tempus Publishing Limited
The Mill, Brimscombe Port,
Stroud, Gloucestershire, GL5 2QG
www.tempus-publishing.com

© Margaret Munro and Archie Foley, 2005

The right of Margaret Munro and Archie Foley to be identified as the Authors of this work has been asserted in accordance with the Copyrights, Designs and Patents Act 1988.

British Library Cataloguing in Publication Data.
A catalogue record for this book is available from the British Library.

ISBN 0 7524 3657 0

Typesetting and origination by Tempus Publishing Limited.
Printed in Great Britain.

Contents

Acknowledgements

We are very grateful to the following persons and organisations for information and the loan of photographs and picture postcards: Ralph Balfour, Elizabeth Blackburn, George Blows, James Bonthron, Kathleen Brown, Rhona Brown, Fiona Crosbie, Elizabeth Cruickshank, Robert Fenley, Tom Forsyth, History of Armadale Association, Arthur Jeffery, Keith Jeffery, Ronnie McCulloch, Valerie McCulloch, Gillian McKinnon, Gordon McRae, Ann McTernan, Margaret Melville, Melville Music Hall, Keith J. Mitchell, Vivienne Nisbet, Portobello Bowling Club, Portobello Burns Club, Portobello History Society, Portobello Library, Portobello Old and Windsor Place Church, Portobello Toddlers Hut, Bob Robinson, Margaret Scott, Sheep Heid Inn, Shepley Family, Margaret Sim, Peter Stubbs, Susan Third, David Thomson, Trotters Club, Ricardo Valvona, Dennis B. White (including permission to reproduce images that first appeared in his now out-of-print book *Exploring Old Duddingston and Portobello*), Archie Young junior.

Finally, we must thank our respective spouses, John and Joyce, for their forbearance during the long preparation of this work.

Introduction

'Welcome to PORTOBELLO Edinburgh's Seaside'. So say the signs on the main roads leading into Portobello. However, Portobello was not always part of Edinburgh. It was a burgh in its own right and a very successful seaside resort. For many people the mention of Portobello brings back happy memories of days at the seaside and the Promenade still attracts many visitors seeking an enjoyable day out.

How did an east coast village in Scotland get such an exotic name? Around 1750 George Hamilton built a house on land known as the Figgate Whins. Hamilton was said to have been a sailor who served with Admiral Vernon on the Panama Isthmus in the campaign against the Spaniards, but was possibly a herdsman. The capture of Puerto Bella in 1739 may have inspired his choice of name for the house he built in this desolate area. Hamilton offered refreshments to travellers using the King's Highway from Edinburgh to the south and east in an area that supposedly was fraught with danger from highwaymen. He also organised horse-racing and visitors discovered the pleasures of the level sands and the fresh air.

The discovery, in the 1760s, of valuable clay beds near the Figgate Burn saw the arrival of industry in the area. William Jamieson, who feued the land, built brickworks, and later tile works, on the banks of the burn. He also established a pottery. Other businessmen were quick to follow suit and a paper mill, soap mill, glass works and other potteries were soon established in the area. Jamieson built a harbour in the 1780s for the use of small boats to import raw materials and export finished goods, but it was short-lived and the harbour silted up with little evidence remaining. Dwellings were built to accommodate the workers and soon a thriving, industrial community was established at the west end of Portobello.

The village of Joppa lay to the east of Portobello. Its industries of quarrying and coal mining had ceased by the 1850s, although salt manufacture continued into the following century, and Joppa became increasingly residential. Both Portobello and Joppa were part of the Parish of Duddingston, but their rapid expansion and the distance to Duddingston Kirk led to the creation of their own parish. The excellent situation and bracing air of

Portobello increased its popularity as a watering place for the residents of Edinburgh and the surrounding areas. The journey initially had to be made by stage-coach and the fare restricted visiting to the wealthier members of society. It became very fashionable and fine villas, often used only as summer residences, were built. Hot and cold sea-water baths were opened in 1805. In 1822, during his visit to Edinburgh, King George IV reviewed several regiments of cavalry on the sand at Portobello. This growth, both as an industrial centre and as a resort, was recognised when Portobello was created a burgh in 1833.

The advent of the railway, in the 1840s, made travel easier and cheaper. A station was built in Portobello and visiting the resort became more affordable for working-class people. Its popularity as a seaside resort continued to increase. The construction of the Promenade was begun and in 1871 a pier was opened, providing places of entertainment and a landing place for boat trips. The pier was demolished in 1917.

Portobello amalgamated with Edinburgh in 1896, although not without significant local opposition. Part of the agreement was that public baths would be built and these opened in 1901. A new Town Hall was also promised and this finally opened in 1914 with a fully equipped stage and auditorium.

Portobello's popularity peaked in the years preceding the First World War and it was arguably the most popular resort in Scotland, particularly with visitors from Glasgow and the West of Scotland. During the Glasgow Fair, the second two weeks in July, special trains ran straight through to Portobello from the west. Between the wars Portobello still drew large crowds and older residents recall holidaymakers sleeping on the beach or grassy areas when guest houses were full. These visitors made their own entertainment by playing music on their accordions or squeeze-boxes late into the night.

After the Second World War, the popularity of foreign holidays grew. Guaranteed sunshine and increasing affordability led to fewer people holidaying at home and Portobello's popularity declined. The closure of local industries, including bottle-works, the power station and the last pottery, forced people to travel further afield for employment. Some may now view Portobello as a dormitory suburb of Edinburgh, but there is a spirit of community valued by residents. People with family connections are moving back to Portobello in the desire to be part of this vibrant community. Much of Portobello is now a conservation area and an active community guard its heritage and protect it against damaging developments.

Although regeneration as a resort is slow to happen, and the potential of the area is not fully realised, the fine sandy beach is cleaned regularly and monitoring safeguards the quality of the bathing water. The pedestrian-only Promenade ensures that Portobello is always a favourite spot irrespective of weather. The Promenade provides a safe family environment and panoramic views to Fife, East Lothian and back towards the city of Edinburgh. Portobello is still a popular place to visit and in which to live.

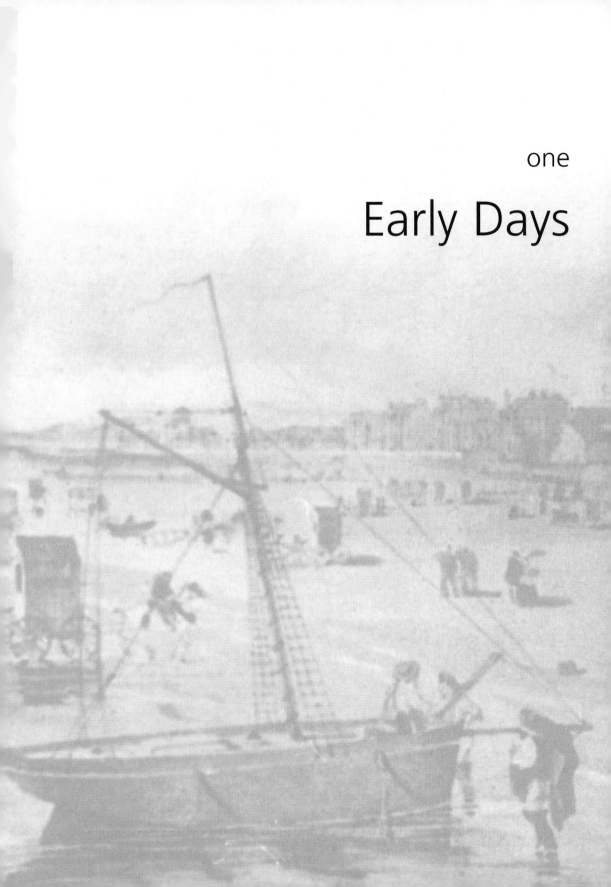

one

Early Days

Portobello grew steadily from the late eighteenth century and by the 1850s had attained a population of about 5,000. Apart from workers to fill the needs of its expanding industries, growing numbers of the middle classes found Portobello, and Joppa, attractive places in which to settle. They were drawn not only by the clean air and bracing sea breezes but also by the fact that there were no local rates to pay. In the period following the Napoleonic Wars large numbers of half-pay officers and their families came to live here. The huddled small houses of the working class on the west of the town were in marked contrast to the elegant middle-class villas with gardens farther east.

Successive Burgh Councils from 1833 overcame a number of early difficulties and by 1896, when Portobello amalgamated with Edinburgh, had created a well run small town with all the amenities of the time. Water and gas supplies had been installed, streets were laid out and links by public transport to Edinburgh established. Law and order were in the hands of the local police and magistrates' court.

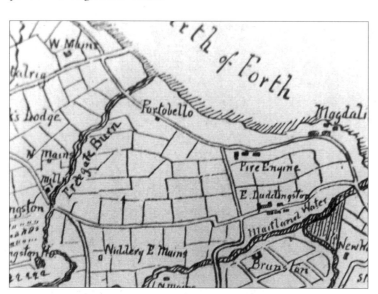

Portobello is represented on John Lawrie's 1766 map of Duddingston Parish by just a single building on the road between Leith and Musselburgh. Further east, Joppa has a cluster of buildings, as does Easter Duddingston, because of their respective already well-established salt manufacture and coal mining industries.

PORTOBELLO HOUSE.

Portobello House stood on the site of what is now 189 Portobello High Street. A newspaper advertisement of the day, in which George Hamilton tried to attract patrons for horse racing on the Figgate Whins, shows that it was certainly occupied by him by 1753. This representation of the house is by William Baird for his *Annals of Duddingston and Portobello* (1898) and may not be wholly accurate.

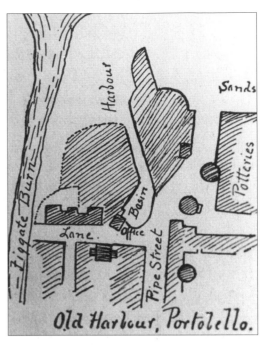

Above left: William Jamieson is on the left in this section of a plate from John Kay's *Edinburgh Portraits.* He was a builder/mason in Edinburgh and, with his father, actively occupied in the development of the New Town. His exploitation of the brick clays was the start of Portobello's growth.

Above right: The harbour built by Jamieson around 1788 fell into disuse by the middle of the nineteenth century due to lack of maintenance and silting up. Until recently, remnants of the breakwater stones could be seen sticking up through the sand at very low tides.

The large harbour breakwaters still jut out in front of the potteries in 1838. Portobello Bay sweeps eastward round past the tower and the by now fairly sizable small town to the salt pans and chimneys of Joppa. Portobello's population at the beginning of the nineteenth century was estimated to be around 300 souls but had expanded to ten times that by this time. The number of houses shown here confirms this.

There are no signs of industry in this 1850 depiction of the sands as a place for genteel middle-class recreation. Bathing machines made their appearance in 1795 and operators had to set out those for males and females at least 60 yards apart or face fines in the Burgh Court. Despite the boat and fishwives, there was no fishing industry in Portobello.

Windsor Lodge Academy in Windsor Place (*c.* 1860) was highly regarded in the community. The *Portobello Advertiser* of 31 July 1868 asserted: '… we are not aware of any private educational institution of equal value in any town in the country of a like extent.'

two

At the
Seaside

In a time when expectations were perhaps lower and pleasures simpler, Portobello's combination of sands, fun fair, concert parties, Promenade and, for a time, pier kept it in the forefront of favourite holiday destinations. It cannot be denied that as a resort Portobello had a few disadvantages; it faced north, its industry was mostly sited in close proximity to the beach and entertainments and the Promenade was bounded by private property for most of its length. This last meant that there was no spare land on which to expand the entertainments, catering and other facilities on offer to trippers and holidaymakers. However, as the picture postcards show, none of these deterred the thousands who came here in the summer months and local people also appreciated what was on offer:

So many places to remember, it's difficult to separate them. The place for pleasure was the Prom with the Fun City where there was the Figure Eight, Helter-Skelter and Cake Walk. Along was Demarco's for real Italian ice cream or, in the winter, saucers of mushy peas and vinegar. There were the donkeys, the Sandcastle King (he had only one leg), the motor boats, the Baths and the Rowing Club. (Margaret H. Sadler, Portobello History Society Collection)

Taking a small boat for a row was as popular a seaside pastime in the 1890s as it is today. There were a number of boating stations on Portobello sands and they were usually marked with a flag. The rights to them were jealously guarded and were passed down through generations of the same families. The best-known family of boat hirers was the Marshalls, whose boatyard was at the foot of Pipe Street.

The original mansion called Coillesdene House was built in the 1880s. The observation tower provided panoramic views over the Firth of Forth and inland over the Lothians. Its Edwardian owner, Mrs Grieve, was an active Suffragette and campaigned vigorously for votes for women. In 1954 her Trustees sold the building to Edinburgh Corporation, who later built an eleven-storey block of flats on the site.

Journeying along Portobello Promenade from east to west, this view overlooks Joppa tram terminus and was taken from the top of Coillesdene House. The pier can be seen stretching out into the Firth of Forth. Also plainly visible on the horizon is the spire of St Philip's Church. This postcard was sent in 1906 and is representative of the view as it was then.

Taken later, this view shows the Venetian Café, which was built at the eastern end of the Promenade. This triangular-shaped building provided welcome refreshments for visitors and residents alike. Looking along the coastline, the pier is no longer there, dating the view to after 1917, when the pier was demolished.

This busy Edwardian scene shows Esplanade Terrace at the eastern end of the Promenade. These terraced villas only have the width of the Promenade and their front gardens to protect them from the waves. In very stormy weather their gardens, and sometime their front rooms, were flooded, although since the sands were restored in the 1970s, the tide no longer comes up to the edge of the Promenade, affording them protection.

In this modern view looking east along the Promenade, the eleven-storey block of flats built on the site of Coillesdene House dominates the landscape. These flats are also called Coillesdene House. On this hot summer day, throngs of people crowd the Promenade, with wind-surfers out on the water.

The eastern end of the Promenade at Joppa offered little in the way of entertainment, with the main attractions at the western, Portobello, end. However, the children's paddling pool was popular and gave children the opportunity to splash about safely when the tide was out, although it filled with water when the tide was in. Unfortunately, this pool has silted up, with little evidence of its existence remaining.

Hamilton Lodge, built in the 1850s, has a dominant position on the Promenade. It was variously used as a dwelling house or a hotel until the end of the twentieth century, when it became a children's nursery. At the time of this photograph it functioned as a hotel, offering easy access to the beach and sands.

Moving further west, the beach is crowded with deckchairs for hire. Notice how formally dressed people are, with the ladies and girls wearing hats and the men in their suits. Left of centre of the photograph the pagoda-like roofs of the bandstand can be seen. The bandstand was very popular and provided entertainment with band concerts and dancing in the ballroom.

The magnificent red sandstone building houses the indoor Swimming Baths, still a very popular venue in Portobello. On the beach a concert party are performing on their portable stage. A performer will go round the audience, on the beach and the Promenade, with a collecting box in lieu of an admission charge. A precarious way to earn your living!

Moving inside the Baths, the men's pond can be seen here, the larger of the two ponds. The Swimming Baths were built by Edinburgh Corporation as part of the amalgamation deal and opened in 1901. They were built to a higher standard than agreed and encouraged fitness as well as swimming, indicated by the provision of ropes and rings.

Above: The Swimming Baths were intended to provide excellent facilities that would enhance Portobello's reputation as a resort and encourage users from further afield. Seawater was used in the pools as this was believed to have curative properties. Turkish baths, a reading room and refreshment buffet were all incorporated into what would probably be described today as a leisure centre.

Left: In the late 1930s Rachel Ritchie, from Aberdeen, was holidaying with her cousins who lived in the Prestonfield district of Edinburgh. They walked to Portobello to spend the day at the seaside and sat on the beach in front of the Clifton Hotel, slightly west of the Swimming Baths. Smiling self-consciously, they are, from left to right: Mr Harry Ford, Harry Ford Junior, Rachel Ritchie and Elizabeth Ford (now Blackburn).

There are always those who prefer to brave the elements and swim in the sea. Despite the bleakness of the day, these swimmers have discarded their clothes and pose before entering the water. Taken during the First World War, this photograph shows the pier in the background shortly before it was demolished for being unsafe.

Crowds are gathering at the entrance to the pier, with several people studying the notices for steamer trips. Advertising was one way of raising revenue and advertisements can be seen for Mazawattee Tea and OXO and, further along the pier, Empire Theatres. An entrance fee had to be paid at the booth before visitors were allowed onto the pier.

What a splendid view to have from your window! The pier, 1,250 feet long and 22 feet wide, can be seen to full advantage, with the restaurant, bar, concert hall and camera obscura clearly visible at the far end. Thomas Bouch, who also built the ill-fated first Tay Bridge, designed the pier, which opened in May 1871. It was the only pier of its kind in Scotland and was both a promenade and amusement pier and a port of call for pleasure steamers. Day trips were popular with visitors and the length of the pier allowed steamers to arrive and depart irrespective of the tide. Unfortunately, the pier was never profitable and following severe storm damage was declared unsafe and dismantled in 1917.

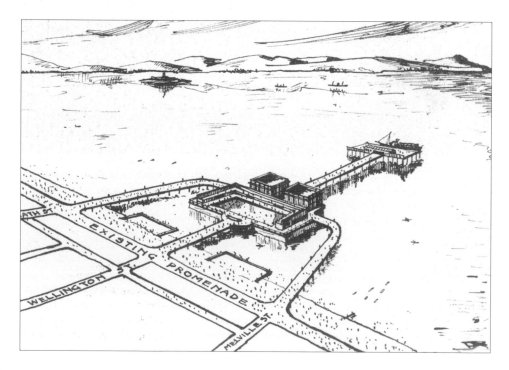

This postcard scene and the following scene are best viewed together as examples of photographic manipulation long before the days of digital photography. In the foreground of this scene are two ladies walking arm-in-arm and a girl gazing out over the water. On the left is a man standing at the head of the walkway down to the beach. It is a calm day. Now look below.

The same scene, the same ladies and the same girl, but the man on the left has disappeared and been replaced by the spray from a stormy sea. The waves are now pounding against the Promenade and the postcard is re-titled 'A Rough Sea'. Photographers frequently manipulated their products in this way to gain maximum benefit from their negatives.

Opposite below: In 1933 Edinburgh Town Council announced ambitious plans for the construction of an open-air pool and a new pier. Local architect Mr Peter Jeffries made this proposal and his initials can be seen in the bottom right-hand corner of the drawing. It appears that several walkways from the Promenade were planned. These would lead to the pier entrance and also the pool. At the far end of the pier further entertainments would be available and what looks like a yachting marina or excursion port of call. However, because of local opposition, the plan to build a new pier was dropped and only the open-air bathing pool was built.

William Kyles and William S. Moir were in partnership in the High Street and Bath Street between 1877 and 1882 and specialised in studio portraits. This is an early, and rare, carte de visite photograph by them of Portobello Pier taken from an unusual viewpoint.

Marlborough Mansions stood opposite the pier and it was an imposing Scottish tenement block. It was built in the 1890s and had distinctive, ornate, wrought-iron railings on the balconies. The interior more closely resembled a hotel, with its long hallways and corridors, than a block of flats. This fine building was demolished in the 1960s when not only the flats but also the ground-floor shops were lost to the community.

Looking east this time, the shop fronts of Marlborough Mansions can be fully appreciated. Everything that the holidaymaker could desire was available. Tearooms were to the left, with Steedman's Beach Bazaar providing spades, pails and other such necessities. MacAlpines Stickybacks seem to have been popular and, of course, the public house on the right provided refreshments as well as billiards for the male members of the family.

Many visitors came down Bath Street to the Promenade and the beach at this point was always very busy. This view looking west to the bottom of Bath Street was taken in 1927. The lady on the left looks very perplexed, while a boy organises the baby in the pushchair. A sign advertises 'ICES', always popular during a day at the seaside. In the distant background the helter-skelter can be seen.

Looking back along the Promenade shows how busy it is. People of all ages are visiting Portobello and perhaps some may have ice cream in Demarco's famous ice cream parlour, indicated by the oval sign. Refreshments could be taken in this elegant café while listening to the resident pianist.

Further west is Shearer's Restaurant, which appears to be built in a private garden. Behind this the Sea Garden Café can be seen with a sign advertising apartments on the gable end of the building. Many holidaymakers rented rooms in houses or small private hotels. The entrance to the pier is visible on the left, dating this postcard to pre-1917.

Above: Boat-trips aboard the *Skylark* were very poplar in the 1950s. With the pier no longer available, boarding her could be precarious depending on the tide, as is seen in this postcard. The water couldn't have been too cold as there are several children enjoying themselves with their mothers seated in hired deckchairs.

Right: This is one half of a stereoscopic photograph taken in the 1890s by an unknown photographer who titled it Portobello Castle. The imposing mansion was in fact built in 1865 by the Edinburgh publisher, Hugh Paton, next to Portobello Tower, which he had bought the year previously. It became an hotel by the beginning of the twentieth century. The old sundial now stands in Brighton Park.

THE BEACH & PROMENADE, PORTOBELLO.

Above: The long unbroken stretch of sand can be seen at its best here. The sand is crowded with visitors, as is the Promenade. On the right of the view is a large tent with a sign advertising Tommy Morgan's Super Entertainment. Concert parties were a very popular form of entertainment in Portobello and Tommy Morgan brought one of the companies who regularly performed here.

Left: Sheila Grant had come to Portobello in August 1949 to meet her mother's family. Frances Roberts, who lived in King's Road, met her husband Cyril Grant when he was stationed at the Marine Gardens during the Second World War and went to live in his home town, Sheffield, when he returned from Burma. The large chimney behind Fun City illustrates the close proximity of indstry to the Promenade.

Taken from the top of the helter-skelter in Fun City, established on the Harbour Green by Billy Codona about 1900, this view looks towards the western end of the Promenade at the foot of King's Road. The art deco frontage of the open-air pool is clearly visible, which dates this view to post-1936. Behind the pool are the four chimneys of the power station.

Taken from the bottom of King's Road, this almost aerial view looks east along the Promenade. Fun City, with its helter-skelter and figure of eight ride, dominates the scene on the right. On the beach, to the left, there appears to be one of the amphibious vehicles, or DUKWS, used by power station employees to check their installations in the Firth of Forth.

Left: Father and daughter are enjoying a stroll along Portobello Promenade, probably in 1954. Isabel McCabe was a student at the University of Edinburgh and her father, Mr John McCabe, came down from their home in Fort William to visit her. Although on a day out, both are formally dressed, with Isabel carrying her gloves in her hand.

Below: Muriel Dodds is struggling to hold onto her large ball here. This group were captured in July 1937 in front of the open-air swimming pool at what seemed to be a popular spot for street photographers. The man on the left of the photograph, wearing the flat cap, is Muriel's father Archie Dodds. The other gentleman is unknown.

Taken almost at the foot of King's Road in the early 1930s, this photograph shows other members of the Dodds family. Muriel Dodds is the baby in the pram being pushed by her mother. Archie Dodds, Muriel's brother, is the boy on the far right at the front. The other lady and boy are friends of the family, possibly Mrs Winton and her son.

Below: This rooftop view shows the big wheel and slide, which replaced the figure of eight and the helter-skelter, in Fun City and was taken in the late 1970s or early 1980s. The roofs seen here belong to the council houses built on land formerly occupied by Buchan Pottery. Two kilns were restored to mark the site of this well-known pottery.

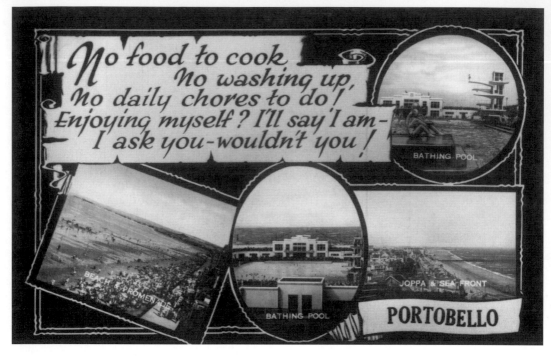

The verse on this multi-view postcard probably appeared on many postcards with the appropriate resort's details inserted. Part of the handwritten message on this postcard says 'Didn't realise Edinburgh was anywhere near the sea'. Visitors are often surprised to find such a long, clean, sandy beach on the outskirts of Edinburgh.

Opposite above: This Valentine's multi-view postcard shows various aspects of Portobello. There is little traffic in the central view of the High Street, although the traffic lights at the Bath Street junction have been installed.

Opposite below: This 'smutty' postcard is typical of comic seaside holiday postcards. 'At Portobello' has been stamped onto the postcard, indicating that these were mass-produced with the resort name inserted.

PROMENADE AND BEACH.

FUN CITY AND BEACH.

HIGH STREET.

PORTOBELLO

THE BEACH.

221303, J.V.

PORTOBELLO AND ARTHUR'S SEAT.

AT PORTOBELLO
THE INTEREST IS IN-TENTS

AT PORTOBELLO.
"Shall I teach you to swim, or will you teach me little mermaid?"

This is a pretty mild example of the traditional seaside postcard by the acknowledged master, Donald McGill.

three

Entertainment

PROM PAVILION

PORTOBELLO

SEASON 1935

For much of the twentieth century Portobello became the summer showbusiness centre of Scotland. There was a host of live entertainment attractions to complement the health-giving properties of the fresh sea air. The beach hosted Punch and Judy, Pierrots and other traditional sideshows, but in addition to these Portobello boasted concert parties and variety companies who took up residence for the summer and put on shows with star performers such as Dave Willis, Donald Peers and Tommy Morgan. This is what Margaret Sadler wrote when recalling her childhood in Portobello:

There's lots of memories; Letta's, roller skating and dancing at the Marines, speedway, church soirees and kinderspiels. Some folk say they were the bad old days; Portobello in my memory never had any.
(Portobello History Society Collection)

Harry Marvello brought the first fully fledged concert party to Portobello in 1905. It was the company that had appeared for him in Ayr the previous year and included his sister, Alice, on the piano. Success was immediate and the seating had to be doubled within a few weeks.

Opposite: The Prom Pavilion was a large marquee set up every summer adjacent to the Promenade at the foot of Wellington Street (now Marlborough Street). It was fitted out as a theatre, complete with lighting and proscenium arch, to host variety shows during the 1920s and '30s. Rather confusingly it changed its name from time to time, being also variously called the Prom Concert Hall and Prom Palace in advertisements. This is the impressively designed programme cover for the Tommy Morgan Company summer season of 1935.

MISS LORA LYNDON
MELVILLE'S ROYAL PIERROTS PORTOBELLO

Left: Lora Lyndon was a member of a large Scottish entertainment family that had toured the country in portable theatres for generations and this Pierrot Company was just one of the many that came to Portobello over the years.

Below: The Tower Pavilion was at the foot of Tower Street (now Figgate Street) and fronted the Promenade. It had been built by Harry Marvello in the space in front of the Tower Hotel, which he had bought in 1906. This photograph was taken in the theatre on the last night of the 1907 summer show and records on the reverse that 'a large number of presents were given … Tom Packer was presented with a cabbage decorated with flowers. Sorry show over.'

Right: Tommy Morgan first appeared in Portobello as a young comic with Andre Letta's company in the 1920s. He was born in Bridgeton in 1898 and was always resolutely Glaswegian in his comedy style. Despite this, he was tremendously popular in Portobello and brought summer shows regularly in the 1930s. He was a bluff, breezy character off – as well as on – stage who died at the early age of sixty.

Below: Tommy Morgan was rarely seen without a cigarette or cigar even for publicity photographs with his large cast outside the tented theatre.

TOMMY MORGAN'S SUPER ENTERTAINERS, 1934

Empire Films   Edinburgh

George Clarkson (far left) may be pretending to be putting cast members through their paces on the Promenade but the performers did really have to have lots of stamina. The local newspaper advertises the show as twice nightly with a nightly change of programme so what with performance and rehearsal there could not have been much rest time.

The Morgan Company did not stint on costumes and production values for its Portobello season. The 1934 show with the same high-quality cast came from successive weeks at the Glasgow Alhambra and Edinburgh's Theatre Royal and the first night was a splendid affair attended by local councillors and guests. The local newspaper reported that the audience 'were taken by storm … and acclaimed Tommy Morgan the most popular comedian in Scotland'. The London revue impresario, C.B. Cochran, relates in his memoirs how he saw Tommy Morgan in a tented theatre in Portobello and thought he was the best comic he had seen in twenty years.

'He [Andre Letta] had a concert party first of all on the Promenade and then in Bath Street for many years – lovely shows he had.' (Mary Olsson, Portobello History Society Collection). The Bath Street theatre was a temporary tented structure. Letta had been a noted conjuror and ventriloquist before putting on his own shows and had performed at Balmoral for the royal family.

Letta had a talent for spotting promising young performers and giving them their chance. Comedian Dave Willis, squatted in front of him during the 1926 show, was one such. He went on to become the highest paid variety performer in Scotland during the 1940s. Another was the singer Donald Peers.

In his later years Andre Letta was a popular Santa Claus in Edinburgh department stores. Peter Nicholls, aged five and from Portobello, had his photograph taken with him at Patrick Thomson's in 1951.

Try this at the Portobello Skating Rink

The *Scotsman* newspaper had advertisements for Portobello Skating Rink in 1876 and 1877 but no location is given. There was roller skating at the Tower Pavilion Rink before the First World War and at the Bungalow before it became a cinema. The Marine Gardens boasted a rink that was 'the largest and finest in Scotland'.

The Cinema Theatre opened on 7 March 1913 at 189 High Street in a building originally built in the 1860s as Portobello's first Municipal Chambers. It is unclear whether or not it operated continuously until the premises were bought by the Portobello Baptist Church in 1919.

The County cinema opened on 30 August 1939 with *Snow White and the Seven Dwarfs*. In 1954 it reopened as the George, after refurbishment and being fitted with stereophonic sound and wide screen, with *The Robe*. Members of the public who queued for the official opening on Monday 22 November were filmed and could see themselves on screen later in the week. It closed its doors on Saturday 15 June 1974.

BATH STREET, PORTOBELLO

Above: The Lees family of photographers had studios in Bath Street for sixty years from 1892. Over the road is the Bungalow, which had had a variety of uses before opening as a picture house in 1912.

Left: The Bungalow's name was changed to the Victory in 1942 and it had lost a good bit of its oriental-style splendour when this photograph was taken a few years later. It did suffer by comparison with its more luxurious competitor along the street and closed in May 1956.

Opposite below: The buildings were transported to Seafield and formed the core of the complex, which was officially declared open by the Lord Provost of Edinburgh on Monday 31 May 1909. The opening day was marred by 'inclement weather' but newspaper reports say that a fair number of people filled the grounds in the afternoon.

CONCERT HALL & BAND STAND.
EDINBURGH MARINE GARDENS, NEAR PORTOBELLO.

The Edinburgh Marine Gardens was an entertainment complex built on 27 acres of ground at Seafield on the western edge of Portobello. It was the brainchild of a group of businessmen who sought to make use of some of the fine temporary buildings built for the 1908 Scottish National Exhibition in Saughton Park, Edinburgh.

Above: The gardens were commandeered by the military in 1914 and only part reopened after the First World War ended. The ballroom reached new heights of popularity between the wars and a motorcycle speedway stadium was built. There was to be no reopening after another government takeover for the duration of the Second World War and the site is now occupied by motor showrooms and a bus garage.

Left: Admission cost sixpence, which gave access to most of the attractions. There was a concert pavilion, skating rink, Bostocks Jungle and American Animal Arena, band court, ballroom and funfair. There were broad avenues for those who just wanted to stroll around the ornamental gardens.

"Bride and Bridegroom," Somali Village, Marine Gardens, Portobello

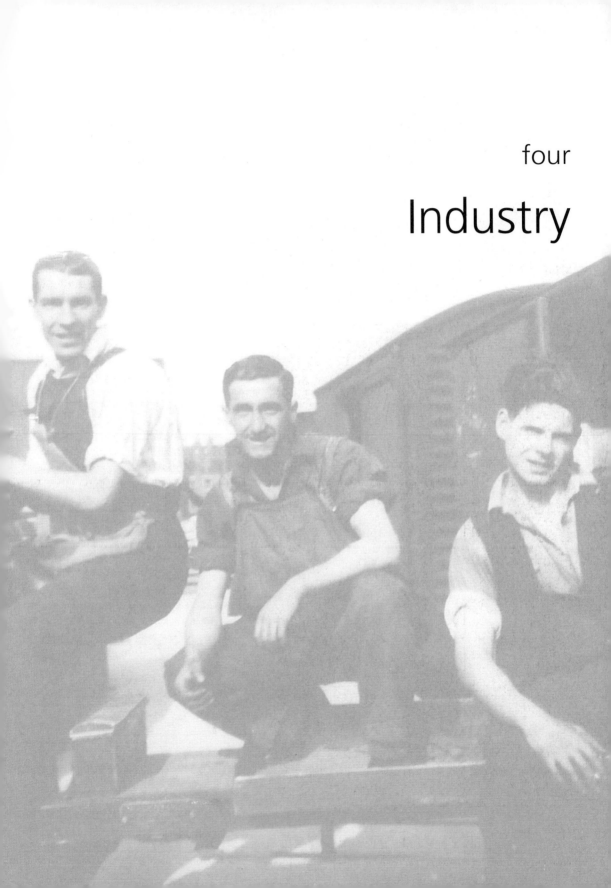

four

Industry

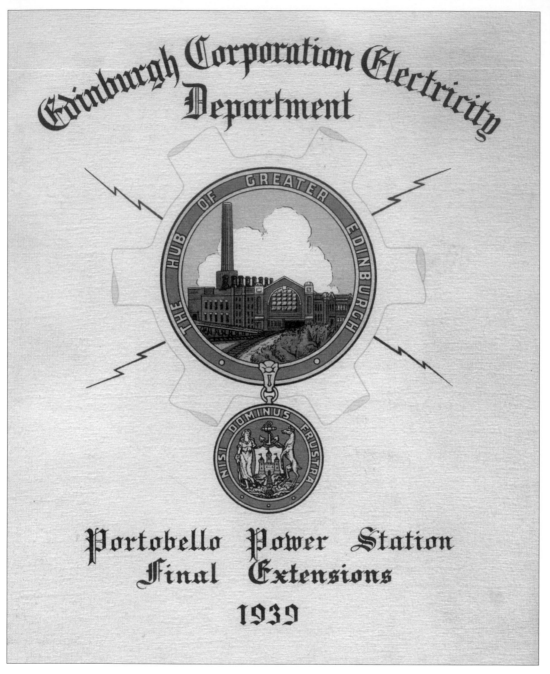

Edinburgh Corporation Electricity
Department

THE HUB OF GREATER EDINBURGH

NISI DOMINUS FRUSTRA

Portobello Power Station
Final Extensions
1939

In 1913 Edinburgh Corporation was advised that its two generating stations at Dewar Place and McDonald Road were nearing the limits of their capacity and a new station would have to be built. The following year over 8 acres of land was bought at the junction of King's Road and Portobello High Street and an additional 24 acres on the west of Baileyfield Road to be used for sidings and coal storage. Building did not begin until after the end of the First World War and it was decided to design and construct a plant with a capacity of 150,000 kilowatts in three stages spread over a number of years. The first stage, with a capacity of 37,500 kilowatts, was officially opened by King George V on 11 July 1923.

*W*hen I was growing up there was a lot of work in Portobello itself. They had the Power Station and they had the paper mill at the top of Bridge Street and there was a small boat yard in Bridge Street itself. There was the cleansing department down Pipe Street and, on the other side, up Fishwives' Causeway they had the glassworks and Skidmore's lemonade factory. On the High Street again, there was Sked's the blacksmiths, which was next door to the tramway depot, where my father worked. There were numerous railway jobs because the goods yard was just up the road and there was Portobello Station, which was very active. The Potteries were at the bottom of Pipe Street and were quite a source of employment for a while. There were also brickworks in the area and the mines. There was a lot of employment available and you didn't have to go into town. (Agnes Bell, Portobello History Society Collection)

Portobello History Society has an ongoing programme of collecting and preserving all material relating to local industry. In 2004, Agnes Bell was recording her memories of growing up in Portobello two generations ago. Portobello Station closed in 1964 but there are still some railway jobs locally and in neighbouring Craigentinny; all the other jobs she listed, and others besides, are gone, living on only in recorded memories and photographs.

The generating station was the property of Edinburgh Corporation but supplied electricity to East and Midlothian as well as the city of Edinburgh. This was distributed by the Lothians Electric Power Company. At first the power station had three short chimneys but a fourth was added later. The landmark 350-foot chimney replaced the short chimneys in 1939.

The only people for whom we have names in this photograph taken on 3 May 1933 are Michael McTernan who is fourth from the left in the third row from the back and the small man with the white moustache on his left, Geordie Foley. 'My father was a boiler scraper – a labourer; he used to come home black. There were no showers or baths at work then.' (Ann McTernan)

Opposite above: Work on the first extension in December 1926 reveals the layers of the famous Portobello Brick Clays and the need for a retaining wall to shore up the High Street embankment. Jones's Garage is on the other side of the High Street going towards Baileyfield Road.

Opposite below: The turbine hall was built on this part of the site. It extended from Rosebank Lane towards King's Road.

Above: The removal of the roof allows a clear view from Rosebank Lane of the No. 1 turbine hall being demolished in 1977/78. The room was 470 feet long and 60 feet wide and three turbines rested on a metal floor.

Left: The 350-foot chimney stack was taken down brick by brick from the top but explosives were used for this final section. Local people turned out in hundreds on 17 December 1978 to witness the dramatic event. A stray piece of girder flew 200 yards and landed only feet away from spectators thought to be safe in Inchview Terrace but this was the only untoward incident.

Above: The original railings fence off the housing estate that was built on the power station site from Portobello High Street. The substantial building on the other side of the street was part of the large Scottish Power estate when this photograph was taken in 1988 but the site has since been sold and redevelopment of some sort is in the offing.

Right: The gas depot in 1957 from the balconies at the rear of 10 Pipe Street. The building in front of the gas holder had been a stable for milk delivery horses but now was used to store bottles of bleach and as a lock-up garage. The gas holder held the supply for local use and was filled up as necessary by pipeline.

These houses in Rosebank Square, photographed in the 1920s, were typical of those built for workers in the area around the Figgate Burn. Rosebank Square was demolished when the open-air bathing pool was built in the mid-1930s. Behind the cottages, and over the Figgate Burn in Bridge Street, is the paper mill.

Paper making began on this site in 1836 and the premises were taken over by Messrs Alfred Nichol & Co. in 1889. They specialised in high-quality paper that was most suitable for books and magazines. This is part of the workforce in 1907. David Hunter is at the bottom right but no other names are known.

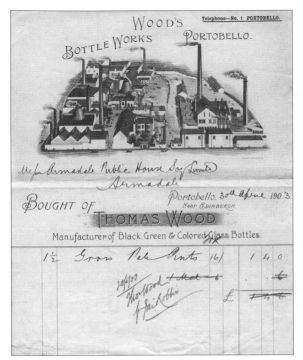

Glass bottle manufacture began in Portobello in 1848 and Thomas Wood joined the industry here from Staffordshire in 1860. In 1866 he started his own firm on the existing site and began an energetic programme of expansion. By 1903 the works had surrounded Mr Wood's large house in Baileyfield Road. Wood also introduced a branch railway from the main line.

The Portobello Bottleworks became the largest and most important in Scotland. The United Glass Bottle Manufacturers Ltd (UGB) bought the firm shortly after the Second World War. UGB closed the works down on 29 December 1967 to concentrate manufacture in Alloa due mainly to the exclusion of Portobello from a 45% investment improvement grant.

William Purves's horses and carts brought sand from the beach to be used in the manufacturing process for many years until this was forbidden for environmental reasons. They also brought waste glass for recycling, as on this occasion in the 1950s.

The ladies are sitting in the glass sorting yard where they separated clear and coloured glass so that each kind could go to its correct furnace. Behind them are the main works buildings.

Right: Archie Young is sitting in the driving seat in this 1938 photograph taken a short way in from the main gate to the bottle works. The names of his companions are not known. Mr Young was working in the Pallet Shop repairing broken pallets at that time but rose over the years to become Sorting and Training Manager.

Below: Many children followed their parents to work in the bottle works. Archie Young junior (apprentice engineer) is standing on the left of the front row of this group of engineers in 1963. Left to right from him are: R. Jefferies, T. Anderson, C. Jones, J. Simpson, A Campbell. Back Row: –?–, –?–, –?–, Jim Campsie, G. Smith, A. Millroy, Alec Campbell, S. Murray. Kneeling: D. Beveridge.

Left: Thomas Wood began importing skilled workmen from Germany in the 1880s. This is the wife and family of Karl Heinrich Mutzke who came to work here with his father and two brothers. All three brothers were interned on the Isle of Man during the First World War when this photograph was taken.

Below: The family was repatriated to Dresden at the end of the war where fifth son Walter was born. He served in the German Army during the Second World War and his Scottish-born brothers were in the British Army. Left to right: Richard, Louisa, Walter, Willi, Oswald, Karl, Karl Heinrich.

Above: The pottery of A.W. Buchan & Co. Ltd is on the left-hand side of Pipe Street behind Fun City. That of W.A. Gray & Sons is on the other side. In the 1920s both firms made utilitarian stoneware such as bottles, preserve jars and whisky flagons but Grays did not survive the recession of that decade.

Right: This is the main yard of Buchan's pottery shortly before the firm moved production to Crieff in 1972 because it could not get a grant to help it modernise and expand in Portobello. Harry Cooper is standing on the left by the door next to his father Danny. Both men were sagger makers. The third man is Harry Preston, who made up the glazes.

Above: The ground-floor throwing shop did not alter greatly over the years. Each thrower had a stall with his potter's wheel situated by a west-facing window. The women standing by the trays of ginger beer bottles were called benchers and made up the balls of clay for the potters.

Left: Philip Christenson is at his wheel making an oil or vinegar bottle in the 1960s. The balls of clay in front of him were weighed out to the precise amount required to make the item.

Arthur Jeffery (*c.* 1960) making a whisky flagon using traditional tools to ensure the correct dimensions. He had to make 350 of them in a day.

After the Second World War Buchan's diversified to start producing hand-painted decorative stoneware in a variety of designs. This has since become very collectable. The decorators, seen here in 1972, are working on plates, mugs and small bowls.

Irene Eyers (later Mrs Irene Forbes), who was head decorator in the late 1960s, painting a large hors d'oeuvre dish.

Ben Slack is showing off in the finishing shop. Finishers put the handles on pots and removed any rough marks by sponging them.

Chris McGarry turning a pot into shape on a lathe in the jolly shop after it had been made in a mould by a 'jollyer'. After this stage the article would go for firing.

Buchan apprentices coming up to the New Year holiday, *c.* 1960. From left to right, kneeling: Rab Laing, Willie Watson. Rear: Philip Christenson, Kenny Mann, -?-, Norrie Palmer.

Portobello, Photographed from an Aeroplane

This aerial view from 1930 shows the concentration of industry at the western end of Portobello compared with the residential layout of Joppa to the east. On the right the chimneys and ovens of the brickworks are clearly visible. The line of Portobello High Street snakes through the middle, with the bend just past the Bath Street junction very obvious.

five

Town and People

Edinburgh has been described as being made up of a collection of villages. Portobello has been part of Edinburgh for a little more than 100 years. Perhaps because of this, and being located on its eastern extremity, Portobello still displays a healthy independence from Edinburgh and a sense of its own identity.

There are still a large number of local sports and social clubs, plus organisations catering for a wide variety of interests. There are families who can trace their local roots back to the middle of the nineteenth century. The High Street does not have the same variety of local shops and businesses as it once had, but this can also be said about Princes Street or any other town commercial centre.

Portobello History Society produced a video in 2004 using recollections, old photographs and home movies to show Portobello not only as a seaside resort but also as a place where people lived, worked and played. The images in this chapter are also chosen to do that.

KING'S ROAD, PORTOBELLO.

Turning into Portobello at this junction, many visitors had their first glimpse of the sea when they looked down King's Road to the Promenade. The coast road from Leith comes in from the left of the photograph. The line of shops on this road is where Peter Braid had his butcher's shop.

This is Peter Braid the butcher, photographed in 1928 standing beside his delivery van. Mr Braid opened his shop in 1923 and delivered in Portobello and as far east as Cockenzie and Port Seton. His son, also named Peter, took over the business from his father, but he has now retired.

Right: Portobello Co-operative Society moved to these premises on the corner of High Street and Pipe Street in 1872. Continuing success led to expansion and the Co-operative bought and developed most of the property between Pipe Street and Bridge Street, enlarging these central premises. Branch shops were established in other areas of Portobello.

Below: John Baillie delivered his bread and cakes to his customers personally. His business was established in the middle of the nineteenth century and he was regarded as the principal baker in Portobello for many years. He supplied bread to Portobello Co-operative Society until it opened its own bakehouse.

Left: The Municipal Buildings of Portobello are shown here in all their 'baronial splendour'. Portobello Town Council built these Municipal Chambers and moved there in 1878. The building also housed the Police Office and various other Council offices. In later years Portobello Public Library was also housed here.

Below: The inside of Portobello Library in the Municipal Buildings is shown here. It was the second branch library in Edinburgh and opened on 1 October 1897 as part of the amalgamation agreement. Initially the library had 4,000 books, but none for children, but the stock was later increased because of high lending figures. Portobello Library moved into a new building in October 1963.

This was the first petrol-driven tender in service in Edinburgh and was used by the firemen of Portobello Fire Station, which was attached to the local Police Station. The appliance, a Humber, was garaged behind the building in Ramsay Lane. These firemen, photographed on 10 June 1908, are, from left to right: D. Thompson, A. Hoare, J. Laird, C.F. Bell and R. Macpherson. Portobello Fire Station closed on 25 September 1926.

The rear of this tenement in Ramsay Lane is a good example of a Scottish tenement. The rounded tower houses the stairwell and open balconies lead to the front doors of the flats. To the left the tenements of Mentone Avenue can be seen, with their fine ornamentation visible on the roofs.

Left: The octagonal tower is probably the oddest building in Portobello. It was built in 1785 as a summerhouse for James Cunningham, an Edinburgh lawyer, using stone and brick from demolished buildings in Edinburgh. Some of the ornamentation is thought to have come from St Andrew's Cathedral.

Below: The citizens of Portobello were promised a new Assembly Hall as one of the conditions of their merger with Edinburgh. This new Town Hall opened in 1914 with a fully equipped stage and auditorium. This photograph, taken in 1922, shows the front of the hall enhanced by low railings and shrubs. These are now gone, with the entrance steps now leading from the broad pavement.

Portobello Town Hall.

Looking west along Portobello High Street, the road is much more enclosed in this view than in later years. Inverey House, on the left behind the railings, has been demolished and the shops on the left have also gone. The High Street has since been widened and the Town Hall is now built on the left, set back from the road.

Still looking west, this 1920s postcard shows that the carriageway has been widened, greatly altering the appearance of the High Street. Both trams and buses are now in use and the traffic lights at the Bath Street junction have been installed. The building with billboards on its gable end was demolished after the Second World War.

Brighton Place, Portobello.

This well-stocked shop was situated on the corner of Brighton Place and Lee Crescent. Passengers from the station walked down Brighton Crescent to the Promenade and beach and this shop appears to stock everything a visitor could desire. Hot and weary travellers could purchase an ice cream further down the street.

Kitty Imrie is pictured here with her parents outside their shop in Southfield Place about 1925. Her father was an unemployed joiner and they moved to Portobello to take over this shop in 1924. Kitty says, 'he was a great golfer and he repaired … he put the stuff on the shaft … the binding and all that and new heads and all that thing.'

Right: J. Williamson, Fishmonger has been trading from this shop at 146 Portobello High Street since 1901. The present owner is James Bonthron, whose great-grandfather married Miss Williamson and thereafter joined her family business. Posing in front of the shop are, from left to right, Laurence Cassidy, Marion Clark, sister of and standing next to her, Archie Bonthron, James's father.

Below: Looking east across the busy junction of Bath Street, Portobello High Street and Brighton Place, a policeman is seen stopping the traffic to let pedestrians cross the road. The shop on the corner is Forsyth the Bakers, renowned for their cakes and confectionery. The business was established in 1847 by John Forsyth and remained in family ownership until 1955, when the premises were sold.

A Masonic Parade marches east along Portobello High Street past Daniel Ross, Bootmakers, 202-208 High Street. Ann Herriot, who worked for him, remembers: 'everybody knew about Danny Ross ... had sympathy for those that maybe were in hard times ... over the years he gave them credit.' (Portobello History Society Collection)

Children wait to cross the High Street at the corner of Regent Street. A. Brand & Sons, Bakers, specialised in making shortbread and gingerbread. Brand was the last Provost of Portobello before its amalgamation with Edinburgh, and he was criticised by many for the part he played in this merger.

J. Williamson, Fishmonger at one time also traded at 310 Portobello High Street. This shop later became part of James Scott & Son, House Furnishers. These ladies seem a mix of customers and fish vendors. James Bonthron, owner of Williamson's at No. 146, believes that the lady on the right is his grandmother.

No. 310 Portobello High Street is now James Scott & Son, House Furnishers. The grocer's shop next door had no family connections, but later became part of James Scott's premises. James Scott also undertook building and joinery work and had a funeral parlour. This business provided great service to the community until it closed in the 1980s.

The tram is heading east into Portobello from Joppa. This is another busy junction at the crossroads of Joppa Road and Morton Street. Joppa residents had their own shops to choose from. A tenement replaced the low house on the right, at the corner of Morton Street, in later years.

The same corner is seen here, with a bus now taking passengers into Portobello and Edinburgh. Portobello Co-operative has opened a branch shop, on the right of the picture, in Joppa. Their mobile shop is parked outside the branch, possibly stocking up with goods before travelling to outlying districts.

Mrs Geaton owned Sadie's, 22 Joppa Road, in the 1950s. She previously had a shop in Portobello High Street, where the Bank of Scotland building now stands, but moved to Joppa and named the shop after her daughter. Ladies' wear was Sadie's speciality and perhaps customers needed re-measuring after eating the sweets they purchased from the shop next door.

Stepping inside Sadie's, Mrs Geaton is standing behind the counter. Sadie often helped her mother in the shop. The shop is typical of the 1950s, with glass cabinets displaying goods and drawers containing much of the stock. In those days customers could purchase almost everything they required locally.

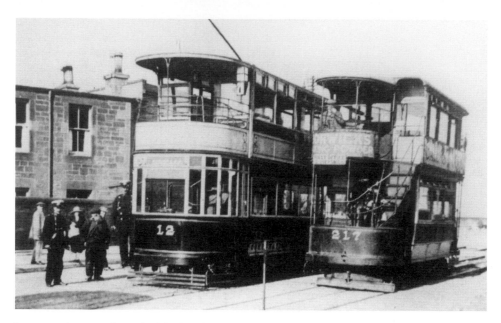

Joppa terminus was the end of the line for the electric tram from Musselburgh and the cable car from Edinburgh. Edinburgh and District Tramways operated their underground cable system from the Edinburgh General Post Office to Joppa until 1923, when they changed to the overhead wire system. Passengers wanting to travel further down the east coast could transfer to a Musselburgh tramcar at Joppa.

Joppa Rocks are a favourite place for children to search the rock pools at low tide. Above the rocks are the buildings of Joppa Saltpans. The houses of the workers are clustered round the Salt Works, which produced salt until the 1950s, making them the longest-lasting producers on the Lothian coast. Only two buildings remain, Rock Cottage, a private residence, and Rockville, now run as a hotel.

Until quite recently, coal was an essential commodity in many houses, providing heat and hot water. One of the Cunningham family is seen here delivering coal in the newly built Coillesdene district. The Cunninghams began business using horse transport, before moving onto using lorries. At one time they had thirteen lorries delivering coal.

A community of nuns linked to the Scottish Episcopal Church ran St Andrew's Home for Girls. Girls in need of care and protection were provided with education and recreation. The girls also ran a very profitable laundry, which contributed to the running costs of the home. The home, however, was forced to close in the 1950s. The property was sold and converted into a hotel.

QUEEN'S BAY HOTEL, JOPPA.

7 minutes by rail from Edinburgh.

Convenient and most comfortable for parents of children attending Loretto School, Musselburgh.

FAMOUS ROCK GARDEN.

Beautifully situated. 9 acres of Charming Grounds.

Tariff from 6/0 per day inclusive

VIEW OF QUEEN'S BAY HOTEL, JOPPA, AND PART OF LAWN.

Charles Jenner, proprietor of Jenners department store in Edinburgh, bought Easter Duddingston Lodge in 1874. He extended the house and created a number of themed gardens in the 7 acres of grounds. The property was sold in 1894 and became the Queen's Bay Hotel.

The hotel offered high-standard accommodation and quiet, secluded well-kept grounds while being within easy reach of Edinburgh. Indeed, it was possible to get to Princes Street in ten minutes in the early twentieth century as the hotel was only a few hundred yards from Joppa Station. This is the dining room.

Several country walks were within easy reach of Portobello. One was from Milton Road, at the top of Brunstane Road, through the farmlands of Brunstane House to the mining village of Newcraighall. This is the 'Roman Bridge', which takes the road over the Brunstane Burn. It is more likely that the bridge dates from the fifteenth century.

Brunstane House owned substantial farmlands and provided a rural retreat for its owners. By the twenty-first century, much of the land had been sold for redevelopment and many houses had been built, encompassing Brunstane House into the City of Edinburgh. A rail link has been provided for these new residents, with few realising the origins of their neighbourhood.

Left: The Roman Catholic Church bought a site at the corner of Sandford Gardens and Brighton Place from the Episcopal Church in 1835. The present church of St John the Evangelist was opened in 1906. This drawing is by the architect Mr J.T. Walford, who lived at 29 Joppa Road.

Below: Portobello Baptist Church moved to this building in Stanley Street in 1912. It had formerly been a private school run by a Miss Shiells. The church moved on again when it bought the premises of the Cinema Theatre at 189 High Street in 1919.

The interior of Portobello Baptist Church dressed for Harvest Thanksgiving Service in 1922.

This church opened for worship on 12 September 1880. It was then a United Presbyterian congregation but through a number of mergers became a charge of the Church of Scotland in 1929. It merged with Portobello Old Parish Church in 1972 and the building is now converted to flats.

Above: The annual Sunday School Picnic was one of the highlights of the year for many children in the inter-war years. The large number attending the Windsor Place Church one in 1922 testifies to its popularity.

Left: The church amateur dramatic section had reformed in 1954 after going into abeyance in the Second World War. As well as performing locally, it competed with distinction in drama festivals and competitions. The name was changed to The Windsor Players in 1967.

Act 3 of *Family Circle*. From left to right: Jim Waddie, Jennie Dodds, Brian Darling, Susan Forrest, Bill Nicol, Valerie Nicholls, Jim Manson. In front: Ann Kennedy, Margaret Smith.

The tenements on the right in Wellington Street (now Marlborough Street) seem to dwarf the Congregational Church opposite on a very quiet day in 1936. The church was founded on 15 September 1836 and although one of the smallest, it has always been vigorous and active in the community. The congregation merged with the United Reformed Church on 1 April 2000.

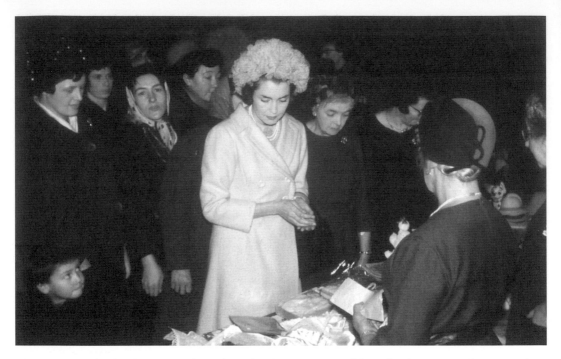

The Countess of Dalkeith (now Duchess of Buccleuch) stops at one of the stalls after opening the Congregational Church's Sale of Work in Portobello Town Hall in 1963.

St Mark's was built at his own expense by a Colonel Halyburton. It opened in 1826 and was consecrated by Bishop Sandford on 21 August 1828. In its early days it was the church for the upper reaches of society and retired army and naval officers.

Above: A St Mark's revue production in the early 1950s. From left to right, back row: Clifford Shepley, Jack Ashworth, Sadie Shepley, Matthew Black. Middle row: Lily Stubbs, Maureen McRae, Joyce Shepley, Joan Scott, Nerissa Black, Margaret Marshall, –?–, Ella Landels, Decima Geaton. Front row: Margaret McCulloch, Moira Stewart, Mike Shepley, James ?, Carla ?, Shirley Shepley (Joan Scott, behind), Hilary Jamieson.

Right: What is now formally called Portobello Old and Windsor Place Parish Church, but is popularly referred to as the Old Parish, opened for worship in 1809. It did not become a full parish church until 1834. Until then it had been a chapel of ease.

The 2nd Portobello Boy Scouts Troop outside the Thomson Hall, Regent Street, 1958. From left to right, front row: Bill Tripp (Scoutmaster), the Revd J.D. Brown (Old Parish Church), Ian Brown (Assistant Scoutmaster), Bob Robinson (Assistant Scoutmaster). The troop was also attached to the Old Parish Church. It was founded in 1914 and ran until 2003. Like so many other organisations for young people, it was the inability to attract leaders that caused disbandment.

Opposite above: Much has been done in recent years to brighten the church interior with new lighting and decoration in pastel shades.

Opposite below: The 2nd Portobello Wolf Cub Pack was attached to the Old Parish Church. Its leaders in the early 1950s were, from left to right: Bill Scott (Cubmaster), Betty Devine, Betty Watt, Isobel Elton, Harold Brown (Assistant Cubmaster).

The Old Parish Church football team at New Meadowbank, *c.* 1950. From left to right, back row: J. McQuillan, B. Anderson, A. Gilchrist, A. Jeffery, G. Paterson, D. Milligan. Front row: B. Milligan, W. Webber, C. Dickson, D. Condie, F. Graham.

The Old Parish Church Youth Club Summer Camp at Comrie in the early 1950s. Douglas Brown is on the extreme right of the second row from the back and Bruce Chalmers is lying on the grass at the front.

St Philip's Church opened for worship on 7 October 1877. It was then within the Free Church of Scotland but became part of the Established Church of Scotland in 1929.

Alexander Runciman, seated centre next to his wife Elizabeth in their back garden in the first decade of the twentieth century, was an Elder at St Philip's for twenty-one years from about 1894. The members of the family group are five daughters, one son and a couple of spouses. From left to right, back row: Elsie, Alex, Jane Kerr, Nan, James Dey, Helen. Front row: Brucie, Babbie.

The Runciman's house, 'Lindenlea', 6 St Marks Place, *c.* 1925. The boy is Jack Runciman, the son of Alex Runciman and his wife Jane, when they visited the family home on a trip back to Portobello from Portland, Oregon.

These boys attended Portobello Higher Grade School in 1918. The boy kneeling extremely straight at the extreme left of the front row is William Elliot. The boy two places to the right is resplendent in full Highland Regalia. Portobello Higher Grade was awarded full secondary status in 1928 and renamed Portobello Secondary School.

Portobello Secondary School moved out of these buildings into a new school in 1964. The buildings were converted into private flats, with the smaller, separate building further down the road, here obscured by trees, converted into a children's nursery school. The new school was renamed Portobello High School in 1975.

Inside a classroom in Portobello Secondary in the 1950s shows pupils self-consciously studying. Agnes Bell remembers, 'We wrote with the pen and nib ... a wee inkwell in the corner of the desk ... It was an honour to be asked to fill the inkwells.' (Portobello History Society Collection)

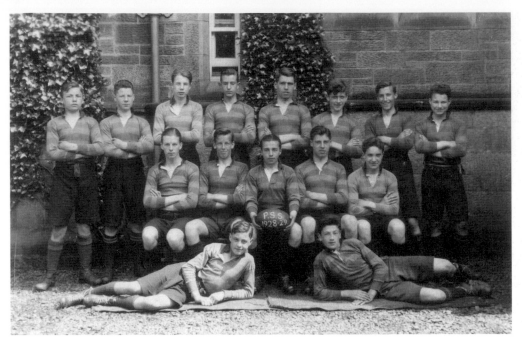

Portobello Secondary School First XV 1928/1929. From left to right, back row: R. Thomson, –?–, –?–, William T. Topp, James W. McKay, David A. Christie, Thomas F. Armstrong, G.M. Scott. Middle Row: A.D. Mackay, C.M.L. Scott, John Archibald (Captain), W.B. Gray, R.F.G. Amos. Front row: J.A.G. Wallace, R. Johnson.

The pupils at Abercorn Lodge School, known locally as 'Illingworth's' after the lady who ran it, appeared in a concert held in Portobello Town Hall in the early 1920s. The Town Hall is a popular venue for local performances and the children, photographed here on the stage, appear to have had a very successful performance.

The pupils at Illingworth's School in Abercorn Terrace are shown here in the garden in 1945/46. The young boy on the far right of the front row is Mike Shepley. The view over the wall looks down to the Promenade and beach.

Towerbank Primary School. End of term, June 1939. The children are all aged between eight and nine years. Betty Watt, now Cruickshank, the owner of the photograph, is in the second front row, fourth from left with the white bow in her hair and wearing a frilly collar.

Towerbank Primary School football team, 1955. Winners of the Gala Cup. Towerbank beat
Peffermill Primary School three goals to one in the final. Mr Allen is on the left and Mr Duncan
is on the right. From left to right, back row: S. Hamilton, G. Dunn, S. Thomson, J. Sutherland,
I. Aitken, R. Parry. Front row: G. Smith, G. Brochty, J. Jenkins (Captain), G. Finlay, G. Krause.

Portobello Burns Club Annual Festival, 26 January 1931. From left to right, back row: Mr John
McVie, Mr Alexander Horn, Mr John MacKie, Superintendent Morren, Bailie Wilson MacLaren, Mr
John Brown, Bailie James Hastie, Treasurer George Sanderson, President D. Lowe Turnbull, the Revd
Farquharson, V.P. Bailie John Hay, Earl Cassillis, Dr Aitchison, Sir Harry Lauder, Secretary William
MacNey, Captain William Balfour, Ex Bailie Grieve. Front row: Mrs John McVie, Mrs William
MacNey, Mrs Morren, Mrs James Hastie, Miss Greta Lauder, Miss Stewart, Lady Margaret Sackville.

Right: The Harry Lauder Plaque is unveiled on 5 August 1995 in Portobello Town Hall. Unveiling the plaque are, from left to right: Jimmy Logan, actor and entertainer, Greta Lauder Fraser, grand-niece of Sir Harry Lauder, and Norman Irons, then Lord Provost of Edinburgh. Members of the Scottish Music Hall Society raised the money for the plaque.

Below: Portobello Tourism Development Association organised a 'Victorian Splash' as a day of fun and entertainment in the late 1970s and early 1980s. Participants were encouraged to wear Victorian costume and join the parade along Portobello Promenade. Having a 'splash' in the water are, from left to right: Margaret Shepherd, Cath Dunlop, John Morrison, Rose Fortune and Margaret Scott.

Members of Portobello Tourism Development Association worked hard in the late 1970s and early 1980s to reassert Portobello as a popular seaside resort. Children's performers provided daily entertainment and play leaders organised children's games. A 'Victorian Splash' was organised and a window-dressing competition was held. This shop window has a display of Portobello photographs and memorabilia. Admiring the display are three committee members, from left to right: Audrey Bullen, owner of a wallpaper and decorating shop, Cath Dunlop, Company Secretary for James Scott & Son, and Eric Langholm, Manager of Murdoch Wight, electrician and electrical retailers.

Portobello Tourism Development Association also participated in the Festival Cavalcade held as part of the Edinburgh Festival celebrations. A 'float' was entered and this one was decorated to advertise 'Fun For All at Porty', with Colin and Doreen Thomson dressed in suitable attire, probably in the early 1980s.

The Sunshine Club of Portobello are seen here participating in either a Gala Day or the Victorian Splash. Established in 1980, founder member and organiser Bernadette Heron is on the right, under the banner, wearing a feather boa and with her face half hidden by a fan. The members of the club enjoy sequence dancing and outings.

Portobello Traders' Association was very active in the community and some members are shown here at their dance, probably held in 1953. The lady with the flowers is Mrs Cameron, who had a dress shop. Behind her is Edith Gregor, who owned Daniel Ross Shoe Shop at the top of Regent Street and second on right, next to her, is Anne Hogg who worked in Daniel Ross's. Most of the other ladies worked in the dress shop. The dance must have been a splendid affair, judging by the ladies' evening dresses.

Left: Jean Tracy was the first Gala Queen in Portobello and was crowned by Scottish actress Rona Anderson in the summer of 1950. Local residents elected Jean as Gala Queen and her consort was Ronnie Lyon. 2,500 children attended the Gala celebrations that year and King's Road, Portobello High Street and the Promenade were gaily decorated with bunting.

Below: The platform party of another Gala Queen, crowned sometime between 1951 and 1955. Tartan dominates the scene here, with the boys looking smart in their kilts. Unfortunately, Portobello no longer has a Gala Day, although many of the communities in the Lothians still carry on this tradition, with the services of brass and pipe bands in great demand.

Right: The public wash-house, or steamie, in Portobello is now used as a Community Centre. Originally run by Portobello and District Community Association, this photograph shows more mature members attending a Christmas party held for around 100 persons in the late 1980s or early 1990s.

Below: The 8th Edinburgh Rover Scout Crew was formed in 1926 and this photograph was taken shortly before they disbanded in 1937. The Crew met in the Tower and are, from left to right, back row: R.D. Angus, G. Simpson, A. Marshall, F. Flemington. Front row: W. Taylor, F. Scott, D.H. Braid (Leader), J.W. Williamson, R. Mackay. Unusually, the Crew were not affiliated to any church.

The 25th Portobello Company of the Boys' Brigade are taking the salute and marching past Portobello Town Hall at the East District Parade in, probably, 1950. Boys' Brigade Companies from Portobello, Newcraighall and Musselburgh all took part and attended the service held in St Philip's Church.

Nurse Chrissie Brown is seen here in the early 1930s at Portobello Toddlers Hut. This playgroup opened in 1929 and is believed to be the longest-running independent playgroup on record. It was originally founded for underprivileged children and was set up by a group of women in Portobello who raised money by holding bridge parties and whist drives.

This street party was held in 1953 at the bottom of Pipe Street to celebrate the Coronation. John Bruce is pictured fourth from the left in the back row, with his friend John standing next to him. Far right in the back row is John's father, Peter Handyside Bruce, with his wife, Isabella Bruce, or Isa Scott, third from right, holding a toddler.

Pipe Street must have been a popular place to hold parties, as the children in this photograph are from the Pipe Street area and are having a fancy dress party to celebrate the Coronation in 1953. Mrs Irene Jeffery, wearing a headscarf, is standing at the top of the steps. Most of Pipe Street has since been demolished and redeveloped.

Above: The Home Guard, 4th Battalion Royal Scots are photographed here in 1943 outside Beachborough House, variously known since as the Temple Hall, Bedford Arms and Dalriada, on the Promenade. The Company Commander was Major Phillips. Several other officers, all in the second row from front are: seventh and sixth from left, Captain MacGregor and Lieutenant Reid, extreme right, Angus Morris, seated second from right, Lieutenant Fiskin.

Left: Melville Music Hall was formed in the early 1970s and their programme presented material in the style of Old Time Victorian and Edwardian Music Hall. Over the years they have raised thousands of pounds for charity. Pictured here are, standing in front of the steps Ginny Spencer, and from left to right, Stewart Williams, Jean Thompson, Sandy Smith, Olivia Begbie, Rosemary Smith, John Carbray.

Above: There were two rowing clubs in Portobello; the Portobello Amateur Rowing Club and the Eastern Amateur Rowing Club. The craft used were called Jolly Boats, which were larger and heavier than the sleek skiffs used on rivers and canals.

Right: Regattas attracted crews from all round the coast. In 1955 this crew from the Eastern Amateur Rowing Club won the Scottish Jolly Boat (Maiden) Championship. From left to right, rear: Doug McLennan, George Peat. Front: Jim Anderson, Tom Forsyth.

Left: Tommy McNama (left) was a well-known skater at the Marine Gardens in the 1930s and won a number of medals. He won the *Daily Record* Glasgow to Edinburgh Roller Skating Road Race Marathon in 1933, winning a gold medal and gold watch, and was second in 1934. That year the winner was 'Curly' Wallace, seen here on the right.

Below: Portobello Thistle Ladies Football Team met in Woods Park and are shown here about 1918. The girl in the centre of the photograph, holding the ball, is Annie Lindsay. The young man third from right in the back row is her brother Jim, who is thought to have trained the team.

Portobello Bowling Club was founded in 1872 and play on their green in Lee Crescent. During their visit to the British Isles in 1952, the Canadian Bowlers Team played the Scottish Bowling Association Team at Lee Crescent. The Canadian Captain, with his stick, is standing on the right and the Scottish Captain, William Jardine, is standing next to him.

Some members of Portobello Amateur Swimming Club, constituted in 1912, play for Portobello Water Polo Team. Often successful in the Scottish Cup, the team won the British Cup in 1997. They are, from left to right, back row: G. Gilhooly, B. Dalgleish, K. Anderson, F. Rutherford, P. Lamb, A. Gilhooly, B. Davidson (Coach), A. Frazer. Front row: R. Valvona (Captain), N. Rutherford, T. Cattley.

PORTOBELLO OPEN AIR BATHING POOL.
Total Cost (approx.) £90,000.
Length 330 ft. Width 150 ft. Area 1·13 acres. Five Diving Stages from 12 ft. to 32 ft. 8 ins. high.
Accommodation for 6000 Spectators. Lockers for 1284 Bathers. Artificial Wave up to 3 ft. high can be developed.

Lord Provost Sir Louis Gumley opened Portobello open-air bathing pool on 30 May 1936. The only other wave-making machine in Great Britain was in an indoor pool in Wembley. The opening gala featured swimming demonstrations, a water polo trial and a display by the Women's League of Health and Beauty.

Maggi Leatham (now Dignal), who lived in the tenements seen at the back of the pool, remembers the announcement made every hour on the hour, 'The waves will be on in just a moment's time. Will non-swimmers at the shallow end kindly keep to the side of the ropes while the waves are on.' (Portobello History Society Collection)

The chutes were a popular feature of the pool and queues would form on hot days of those wanting a slide. The pool was open from May until September every year until war broke out in 1939. During the war it was camouflaged to prevent it acting as a marker for German bombers. It re-opened on 1 June 1946.

The water beneath the high-dive was 15 feet deep. Hot water was provided for the pool by the neighbouring power station. When it closed in March 1977, this supply was lost. The pool ran at a loss throughout the 1970s and there was little money for repairs. The pool finally closed in 1978.

There were many galas and treasure hunts held in the pool. Evening galas often ended with fireworks and in this postcard they illuminate the fine art-deco architecture of the function suite. Unfortunately these buildings were not placed on the register of listed buildings and they were demolished in 1988.

Aptly titled 'The Call of the Seaside', this postcard, postmarked 15 August 1939, portrays three of the attractions that were to be found at Portobello: the sandy bathing beach, the funfair and the open-air bathing pool. The sandy beach is still there, with cleaner water than in 1939, and Portobello is still an enjoyable destination for a day out.

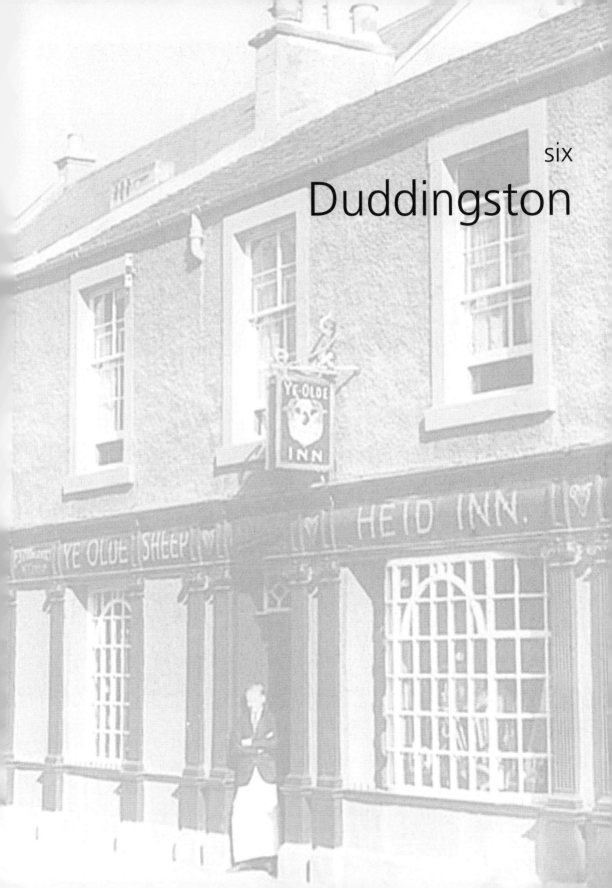

The Revd William Serle was the longest-serving minister in the history of Duddingston Kirk. He was born in East Linton, East Lothian on 18 November 1866 and received his early education at the Free Church School in that village. After graduating as a Master of Arts at Edinburgh University in 1889 he became a Bachelor of Divinity in 1892. He had spells as Assistant at Peterhead, Northesk and St Aidan's, Edinburgh before being ordained at Duddingston on 16 April 1903. He died on 5 April 1947 aged eighty.

There are two theories as to how the place name Duddingston came about. One has it that it derives from the Gaelic, meaning the place 'on the sunny side of the hill', but it is more likely to originate from a family named Dodin that appears in twelfth-century charters as 'Dodin of Dodinstun'. Spellings varied in those early years and it was often rendered as Dodingston but eventually became standardised in the form we know today.

In this chapter we deal only with that part of the parish previously known as Wester Duddingston, which is the area around the present village by the loch; the other villages, Portobello, Joppa and Easter Duddingston are dealt with in other chapters.

'Arable farming provided almost all the employment but the New Statistical Account entry of 1843 notes a steady decline in population and an increase in empty cottages due to new farming methods.' The author of this entry did not foresee the changes that overtook his parish from the late nineteenth century. The improvement in road, and then rail, communication with Edinburgh brought urbanisation. It was slow at first but gathered pace during the inter-war years of last century and as Agnes Parry writes:

At the end of the Second World War the pace of change quickened, the farmlands of Northfield, Southfield and Eastfield gave way to regiments of bungalows interspersed with Council housing … In August 1950 the mills [sic] wheels at Duddingston turned for the last time. (The Kirk at Duddingston through the Ages, page 41)

Duddingston may now be a suburb of Edinburgh but it has two institutions that help it retain an undeniable village community spirit. These are an historic parish kirk and equally historic village pub.

DUDDINGSTON VILLAGE AND JACOB'S LADDER FROM KINGSTON, EDINBURGH. 9.

Jacob's Ladder is the steep, stepped pathway on the left of the photograph by which it is possible to walk over the lower slopes of the hill from Duddingston to the Meadowbank gate to Holyrood Park. Although close to Edinburgh geographically, Duddingston village was fairly isolated due to poor roads.

Duddingston Kirk dates from the twelfth century. The hexagonal building is now the Session House but was originally a watch tower that was manned at night to protect recently filled graves from being raided by body snatchers looking for cadavers to be used for anatomy lessons at medical schools in Edinburgh.

These old cottages stood in the lane at the top of The Causeway leading from the main road. The lane at one time connected to one of the old roads to Edinburgh. The village police station was once located here.

The cows were allowed to make their own way from the fields along The Causeway, which they entered by the lane at the eastern end, to the dairy for milking.

The milk cart is standing at the entrance to Duddingston Dairy at the western end of The Causeway. The entrance is clearly identifiable today by the stone tracks laid for the cart wheels to run on to prevent them sinking into soft ground.

Above: Duddingston House was built between 1763 and 1768 for the 8th Earl of Abercorn. The architect was Sir William Chambers who also designed the building in St Andrew's Square, Edinburgh that is the Head Office of the Royal Bank of Scotland. It was hardly ever lived in by the Abercorns, who preferred their estates in Ireland and was let out or empty for long periods.

Left: The house and grounds were taken over by the army during the Second World War and, after they left, the Nissen huts remaining were used for a while to house homeless families. Eventually, the house was bought in 1960 by Mr Edward Gladstone who painstakingly carried out a programme of restoration. This is one of the original fireplaces with Dutch tiles, which has been returned to its original splendour.

Curling on Duddingston Loch

With Season's Greetings.

Duddingston has an honoured place in the history of curling. Duddingston Curling Society was formed in 1795 and the rules drawn up by its members in 1803 to regulate the game and avoid disputes have been adopted as the basis of the rules that govern the sport internationally today. The advent of indoor rinks and warmer winters has meant that curling has not been seen on the loch for many years but the octagonal tower once used as a clubroom still stands.

Duddingston Loch.

Postcards were often used to send messages before telephones became widely owned. Mercifully, few were as dramatic and serious as the one on this card posted in February 1903. This is part of it; 'I had a very narrow escape … a Divine deliverance from a tragic death. I got well kicked by the horse on the left leg; the lorry wheel took out a piece of the calf of the right leg and laid bare the bone!'

The pupils of Duddingston School with their teacher, Miss Reith, *c.* 1923. In the middle row, third from the right, is Hettie Bell, daughter of the foreman at Duddingston Mill.

Gardening lessons were part of the curriculum around 1910 but the children appear to be dressed more for the camera than hoeing or digging. The schoolmaster's fine house was demolished in the 1980s. The old school buildings behind it were replaced by wooden 'huts' which eventually made way for the present primary school building in 1955.

There was a forge at Duddingston Mills for generations, which operated under the name of Thomas Horsburgh. The man on the left is Peter Wood and on the right is John Meikle.

The Aitken family worked the mill at Duddingston for over sixty years until its closure in August 1950 but there had been mills on this site beside the Figgate Burn for about 600 years. This is the mill building and granary about 1915. Each cart required two horses to pull it up the steep lane to Willowbrae.

After closure the mill site was eventually acquired by developers for housing in 1984. Four years later the mill building's conversion into an apartment block is almost complete.

David Bell, the mill foreman, photographed with his dog aruond 1915 outside the mill office. The view of the mill building behind the office shows off its 'Dutch barn–style' roof.

This thatched cottage, photographed about 1910, belonged to Northfield Farm, which was part of the Duddingston Estate. It housed two families and stood in the middle of the present Northfield Broadway close to Northfield Community Centre.

The Sheep Heid Inn is a very famous institution in the village of Duddingston. This external view, taken in 1935, shows a very anglicised version of the pub's name, later replaced. The name derives from a local delicacy, singed sheeps' heads, which were served boiled or baked to hungry travellers.

This view of the bar in The Sheep Heid Inn was taken in 1935. Described as 'Scotland's oldest pub', its origins are believed to date back to 1360. Very few alterations have been made to the bar other than the removal of the jug bar, to the rear on the right, and the sawdust spittoon, on the floor round the foot of the bar.

These customers are enjoying the sun in the beer garden to the rear of The Sheep Heid Inn. This photograph was taken in 1935 and the balcony has since been restored, with tables now available on it to enjoy a meal. Barbecues are held in the central area, now covered, at weekends.

This bowling alley is a long-standing feature of The Sheep Heid Inn and is built at the rear. Shown here in 1935, few changes have been made and it is still necessary for someone to replace the skittles after they have been knocked down.

Around 1882 The Trotters Club was formed and adopted The Sheep Head (as it was then known) in Duddingston as their home. Members, shown here in 1904, played skittles in the alley there, a tradition which King James VI of Scotland is claimed to have started. He is also said to have presented a 'Sheephead' to the hostelry.

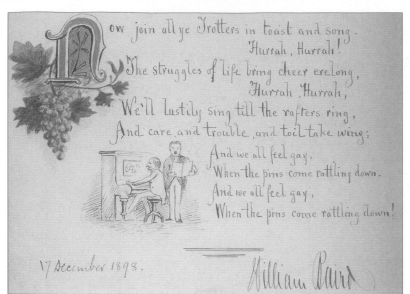

Now join all ye Trotters in toast and song.
'Hurrah, Hurrah!'
The struggles of life bring cheer ere long,
'Hurrah, Hurrah,'
We'll lustily sing till the rafters ring,
And care, and trouble, and toil take wing;
And we all feel gay,
When the pins come rattling down.
And we all feel gay,
When the pins come rattling down!

17 December 1898.

William Baird

The Trotters Club journals contain many examples of the artistic and poetic skills of its members. This effort by William Baird appears to be designed to be sung to the tune of 'When Johnny comes Marching Home'.

Five distinguished members of the Trotters in 1917. From left to right: M.T. Anderson (aged seventy-four), James Patterson (aged eighty-seven), William Baird (aged seventy-four, author of *Annals of Duddingston and Portobello*), John McArthur (aged eighty, founding secretary), Alexander Brand (aged eighty, last Provost of Portobello).

The menus produced for the Trotters Annual Dinners were works of art, employing the skills of the many talented members. This menu for 1912 shows Arthur's Seat and Duddingston Loch, with sheep, symbolising members of the club, in the foreground. The members also wrote many poems and songs celebrating club activities and commemorating each other.

Left: William Baird was the Agent (Manager) for the Clydesdale Bank in Portobello and a prominent, active member of the community for many years. He was a Fellow of the Society of Antiquaries of Scotland and an enthusiastic local historian. His *Annals of Duddingston and Portobello* (1898) is still the required starting point for anyone setting out to study the history of the area.

Below: The Balfour family practised medicine and cared for people in the Portobello and Duddingston area for several generations. The family of Dr John Balfour, who died in 1944, can be seen here. Ritchie, Dr John's chauffeur, is holding the head of Dora, the horse. Seated side-saddle on the horse is Edie, Dr John's daughter, watched over by her brother Andrew.

Right: Betty Ford (now Blackburn), standing, is playing with two friends on the beach at the bottom of Bath Street around 1933. The buildings behind them would be familiar to three generations of visitors and residents.

Below: In 2005 this ultra-modern apartment block was built on the corner of Bath Street and the Promenade. Will it be a landmark for as long as Marlborough Mansions and the buildings it replaced?

Other local titles published by Tempus

Kirkliston
KIRKLISTON LOCAL HISTORY ARCHIVE

This unique collection of over 220 old photographs of Kirkliston, including many which appear here in print for the first time, has been compiled by the Local History Archive from a wide range of sources, including the collections of many local schools, churches, societies and private individuals. The book tells the story of the community, featuring local people and such distinct local elements as Marandola's ice cream and the annual Children's Gala.

0 7524 1131 4

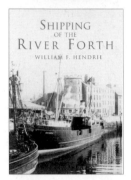

Shipping of the River Forth
WILLIAM F. HENDRIE

For thousands of years the River Forth has been used by man. From Stone Age shell middens to the Roman port at Cramond there is much evidence of man's use of the river and its estuary. From the fishing harbours along the Fife coast to the ports of Grangemouth, Leith and Granton, as well as the naval bases at Rosyth and Port Edgar, the maritime history of the Forth is covered here.

0 7524 2117 4

Hibernian Football Club 1875-1975
PAUL LUNNEY

This collection of almost 200 photographs and items of memorabilia traces the history of one of Scotland's most famous clubs, from its foundation in 1875 through the first 100 years of its history. Some of the featured highlights include Hibs' achievement of being the first East Scotland team to win the Scottish Cup in 1887, through Championship success in 1948, 1951 and 1952, to the 1970s Turnbull era.

0 7524 2170 0

Bannockburn 1314
ARYEH NUSBACHER

Recent scholarship has illuminated one of the most exciting battles of Scottish history, showing it to be as historically significant as it was romantic and bloody. This book carries the reader through the politics and plans of a military campaign of the Middle Ages, including the logistical sinews of war, the drama of court intrigue, and the violent clash of soldier against soldier. This book opens the files on a year's preparation for a massive English invasion of Scotland.

0 7524 2982 5

If you are interested in purchasing other books published by Tempus, or in case you have difficulty finding any Tempus books in your local bookshop, you can also place orders directly through our website

www.tempus-publishing.com